Providence and Liberty

Selected Passages from Frédéric Bastiat

Providence and Liberty

Selected Passages from Frédéric Bastiat

Second Edition

Translated with an Introduction by Raoul Audouin

Foreword by Robert A. Sirico

Preface by Leonard Liggio, Jacques Garello, and Samuel Gregg

*I trust entirely the wisdom of the laws established by
Providence and, for that very reason,
I put my faith in liberty.*

—Frédéric Bastiat

Contents

Foreword

The term *classical liberal* is a deeply ambiguous phrase. It is often linked with individuals such as Lord Acton and Alexis de Tocqueville, whose belief in freedom is incomprehensible without understanding their religious background and beliefs. For such men, the true liberal is one who grounds his belief in freedom in the idea of a God who created the human person whose very destiny is freedom.

Unfortunately, the word *liberal* is also affiliated with philosophers such as Jeremy Bentham and John Stuart Mill, both of whom were profoundly deterministic in their understanding of life and ultimately incapable of articulating a coherent philosophy of why it is good for man to be free. It is thus understandable that many associate "classical liberalism" with a thorough-going secularism, in the sense of an agonistic or atheistic view of man rather than an authentically Christian humanism.

The secularism of which we speak is one that holds that, in the final analysis, human life is merely the sum total of so many randomly related atomic parts, and that the beginning and end of the human person is to be found in his materiality. Christian humanists, by contrast, regard man as being made in the image of God. This, they believe, is the only basis for man's rights, his duties, and ultimately his call to authentic freedom that meets the demands of faith in the

Revelation that is Jesus Christ but also the requirements of right reason itself.

Certainly, there are many today who recognize the value of the English, Continental, and American classical liberal traditions, but who persist in simultaneously denying that man has a transcendental dimension. Frédéric Bastiat was, however, one believer in freedom who rejected atheism, agnosticism, and—eventually—the tendency to Deism. It was precisely Bastiat's firmly held belief, as a Christian of the Roman Catholic tradition, in a purposeful God who took on flesh in the Person of Jesus Christ that led him to conclude that the natural order, left peaceful, would ultimately display the wisdom of the God who is its origin. The *truth* that is God is, in Bastiat's view, the only solid foundation for freedom and the only reasonable basis for explaining why man should be free.

Most English language readers, if they are familiar with Bastiat at all, know him through a slender yet potent work entitled *The Law*. Somewhat fewer are aware of the religious dimension of his thought and how much Bastiat's ideas about the social and economic order were shaped by his acceptance of the central tenets of orthodox Christian belief. This included the belief that Christians can know moral truth through reason, a view that is often called "the natural law tradition." Here we find the roots of Bastiat's way of reasoning and his understanding of the character of man's dominion over the material world.

To view Bastiat's *The Law* in isolation from his many thoughts on such subjects is not only to lose a sense of its context but also to fail to do justice to the depth and complexity of his thought, for while Bastiat would have agreed with Lord Acton that to be a true liberal is to believe that liberty is "the highest political end of man," Bastiat's religious commitments—and for that matter, Acton's—prevented him from thinking that the political and economic fruits of liberty are the total end of man. While they are necessary conditions for the emergence of a free society, for Bastiat they are not sufficient for a society characterized by the moral good that we call habits of virtue.

As readers of this book observe Bastiat explaining over a period of years his religious ideas and principles, they will soon discern that Bastiat rejects the idea of liberty as a self-justifying principle—as a floating abstraction at best—and the premise for a tyrannical regime at worst. Ultimately, for Bastiat, liberty is rooted in the *real*; that is, the truth about man where we also find the moral law that Christians believe to be inscribed into man's very reason itself, but which has been definitively revealed to us in the life, death, and resurrection of Jesus of Nazareth. In this belief lies the ultimate salvation of the tradition of freedom from those who would distort it into anarchism, as well as those who would use the lie that there is no truth as an excuse to plunge mankind into a world of tyranny and terror.

—Rev. Robert A. Sirico

Preface

Frederic Bastiat: A Journey of Faith and Reason

Frédéric Bastiat was born on June 30, 1801, at Bayonne in the Department of Landes on the south Atlantic coast of France. His mother died when he was seven, and his father passed away just two years later. An only child, Bastiat went to live with his paternal grandfather and his spinster aunt in Mugron. Between 1815 and 1818, he studied philosophy and languages—Spanish, Italian, and English—at the well-known College of Soreze founded by King Louis XVI.

Perhaps the most significant intellectual event in the young Bastiat's life was his reading, at the age of nineteen, Jean Baptiste Say's major work, *Traite d'Economie Politique* (1803/1814). "I have read the *Traite d'Economie Politique* by Jean Baptiste Say, an excellent and methodical study," he wrote to a college friend.

Say's thought continued to influence Bastiat throughout his career. When Bastiat founded his periodical, *Le Libre-Exchange*, the masthead carried Say's famous "Law of Markets" as its motto: *Products Exchange for Products*. As the Bastiat commentator, Dean Russell, observes:

> Throughout his speeches and articles, Bastiat's favorite themes were taken from Say—products exchange for products; services exchange for services; production creates its own purchasing power; general overproduction" is a myth; the mercantilist

> concept of a "favorable" balance of trade is non-sense; services have real value in the same sense that material products have value; selling is a form of buying, and vice versa; and various combinations of (and deductions from) those principles. Say was also probably primarily responsible for Bastiat's constant claim that all permanent distortions in the marketplace are caused solely by governmental interference—and that harmony would reign in a free market where the government confined its activities mostly to keeping the peace and punishing fraud.[1]

Bastiat worked in his family's banking and commercial firm for six years. He retired to his grandfather's estate at Mugron, which he inherited following his grandfather's death in 1825. Bastiat's next-door neighbor, Felix Coudroy, became his friend and intellectual partner. Originally a disciple of Statist thinkers, Coudroy came to share Bastiat's philosophy of freedom.

The subject of freedom and State power was at the heart of many of the political debates that characterized early and mid-nineteenth-century France. Indeed, it is difficult to overestimate the degree of political tension that dominated France during this period as a consequence of the social, economic, and intellectual turmoil unleashed by the French Revolution. Between 1788 and 1830, France's political institutions shifted from the powerful monarchy inherited from Louis XIV, to the constitutional monarchy created by the events of 1789, the Jacobin republic (1792–1794) of State terror, the moderate—albeit corrupt—republic of the Directory (1794–1799), the military dictatorship and Consulate (1799–1804) of General Napoleon Bonaparte, the First Empire (1805–1814) of Napoleon I, the restored Bourbon Monarchy (1815) of Louis XVIII, the temporarily resur-

---

[1] Dean Russell, *Frederic Bastiat: Ideas and Influence* (Irvington-on-Hudson, New York: Foundation for Economic Education, 1965), 18.

rected Napoleonic Empire (1815), to the again-restored
Bourbon Monarchy (1815–1830) of Louis XVIII and then of
his brother, Charles X.

Nevertheless, underlying this evident instability of constitutional arrangements, certain constants prevailed.
Perhaps the most ominous was the ongoing centralization of
state power. Far from liberating the people of France, the
Revolution had swept away the intermediate associations
and civic institutions (Edmund Burke's "little platoons")
that had, to a surprising extent, limited the *ancien régime*'s
powers.[2] Napoleon's organizational reforms had completed
this centralizing process, leaving the State apparatus with
few real constraints on its administrative powers. This centralization of State power in France was underlined by
Alexis de Tocqueville in two of his most important works,
Democracy in America (1835/1840), and *L'Ancien Régime et La
Révolution* (1856). Significantly, centralization was not opposed by royalists, republicans, or Bonapartists. Each
grouping was anxious to use the State to bolster its own
power, to crush its political opponents, and to subordinate
the law to the realization of their particular ideological ends.

The most immediate political struggle that characterized
Bastiat's youth, however, was the conflict between the
restored Bourbon monarchy, specifically that of King
Charles X and his supporters, and liberal constitutionalists
such as Francois Guizot. This climaxed with King Charles's
attempt to suspend the 1815 Charter that established certain constitutional parameters in Restoration France and to
replace it with rule by royal ordinance. The result was the
July Revolution of 1830, which ended in the exile of the
senior branch of the Bourbon dynasty and the installation of
the junior Orleanist branch, in the person of Louis-Philippe,
on the throne. With the establishment of the July Monarchy,

---

[2] See Samuel Gregg, "In the Shadow of the Reign of Terror," *Policy*, vol. 16,
no. 1, 2000: 43–47.

Bastiat was appointed a justice of the peace. In 1833, he was elected to the General Council of the Department of Landes, serving in this position until his election to the National Assembly in 1848.

A Constitutional Tradition

Bastiat was not, however, simply an active participant in the politics of his time. He actively contributed to French philosophical reflection about the nature of freedom and its implications for the social, economic, and political order. After studying Say's work, Bastiat read authors ranging from Physiocrats such as Quesney and Turgot, to Adam Smith and Destutt de Tracy. An important disciple of Say and Desutt de Tracy was Charles Dunoyer (1786–1862), with whom Bastiat was to work closely in Paris in the 1840s. Bastiat was profoundly influenced by Dunoyer's thought as well as by the ideas of his colleague, Charles Comte. Bastiat had, for example, subscribed to *Le Censeur*, which Dunoyer and Comte published in Paris from June 1814 until September 1815 when the journal was suppressed by the ex-Jacobin regicide and minister of police for successive Republican, Napoleonic, and Restoration governments, Joseph Fouche.

In their enforced retirement, Dunoyer and Comte moved beyond expositions of liberal constitutionalism to engage in deeper historical and sociological analysis of society. In this connection, three authors gained their particular attention. One, not surprisingly, was Say. The second was the historian, Comte de Montlosier (1755–1838), who wrote pioneering works on the rise of the French middle class during the Middle Ages. The third was Benjamin Constant (1767–1830). A member of the Chamber of Deputies, Constant combined an active political career with a vigorous intellectual life and regularly wrote on contemporary issues such as constitutionalism and freedom of the press, as well as longer pieces on the course of French and European history.

Constant's particular method of historical analysis was to focus on the perennial theme of liberty versus power. On this basis, Constant rejected the pagan State worship of the ancient world and welcomed the liberty associated with modern commercial society. Interestingly, he (like Bastiat) associated the recognition of the justice of private property arrangements within commercial societies, with Christianity's ongoing influence upon European culture. Constant thus saw the necessity of refuting "two false propositions": The first was the notion that "religion is the natural ally of despotism;" the second being the belief that "the absence of the religious sentiments [is] favorable to liberty." As noted by the editor of Constant's political works, Edouard Laboulaye (1811–1883): "To proclaim that God has rights is to tear asunder the unity of despotism. There is a germ of revolution which separates the ancient from the modern world."[3] A similar theme is echoed in Lord Acton's "The History of Freedom in Christianity."[4]

Like Constant and Acton, Bastiat was also a committed Christian, though, in his youth, he initially wrestled with the question of belief. In later years, Bastiat consciously integrated his religious faith into his thinking about the social and economic order. For Bastiat, the order of the divine was not just the "unseen." Like other Christians throughout the ages, Bastiat believed that much of the divine order—and thus, much of the truth about God and man—is discernible through human reason. We should not therefore be surprised to find that the theme of *natural law* resonates throughout Bastiat's writings on economics and jurisprudence.

---

[3] Introduction of Laboulaye to Constant, *Cours de politique constitutionelle*, 2 vols. (Paris, 1861).

[4] *Essays in the History of Liberty*, vol. 1 (Indianapolis, Ind.: Liberty Classics, 1985), 29–53.

Free Trade and Natural Law

In 1844, Bastiat wrote a lengthy article on the role that tariffs would play in the future of the English and French peoples. Published in the October 1844 issue of *Journal des Economistes*, the piece made Bastiat's name familiar throughout intellectual circles in France. Dunoyer and others immediately drew him into their group of Parisian economists.

Bastiat's intellectual contacts were not, however, limited to France. He was also acquainted with Richard Cobden, the English parliamentarian who led the successful struggle for the repeal of England's protectionist Corn Laws. Inspired by the vigor and success that Cobden brought to this cause, Bastiat wrote a book simply entitled *Cobden* in 1845 and inaugurated "The Association for Freedom of Exchanges" in Bordeaux. The Association had a small membership, and Bastiat sometimes felt a sense of powerlessness and lassitude. Nevertheless, ideas on free exchange spread, reaching their zenith with the conclusion of the French-English commercial treaty. Appropriately, it was Michel Chevallier, an admirer of Bastiat, who led the French negotiators.

Bastiat's very readable economic writings are based on the theme of humanity's natural economic and social harmonies. Bastiat demonstrated that competing human interests could be reconciled in a free society where government is confined to preventing crimes against persons and property, and obstructing those who wish to live at the expense of others. His economic ideas received considerable recognition from a variety of sources. In 1877, for example, Gioacchinno Cardinal Pecci—better known to the world as the future pope, Leo XIII—publicized Bastiat's concept of natural harmony among the true interests among men in their social and economic relations. Speaking of Bastiat, Pecci declared: "A celebrated French economist has clearly explained the many benefits that society brings to man, and that marvel is worthy of our attention."

In the free market, Bastiat contended, no one is able to accumulate capital (except for gifts) unless one provides a service to someone else willing to exchange money for the service or product. Violations of this principle disturbed him. Some of Bastiat's most forceful essays concern the theme of *A* manipulating State power to take money forcibly from *B* to support *C*. This concern underlies one of his better-known axioms: "The State is the great fiction by which everybody tries to live at the expense of everybody else." The same principle is reflected in Bastiat's observation that "Everybody wishes to live at the expense of the State, but they forget that the State lives at the expense of everybody."

Still, Bastiat's greatest contribution to the tradition of freedom was his book, *The Law*. Written in 1850, shortly before his death in Rome (where his tomb is in the Church of Saint Louis, Roi de France), the title of this book underscores the primary reference point from which Bastiat derived most of his ideas. This may be summarized in the following manner: There are laws that may be known by fallible human persons through not only Revelation but also right reason; and the violation of any of these laws inevitably results in social, economic, and political disharmony. "When human institutions infringe on divine laws," Bastiat wrote, "not only error but Evil is the result." Bastiat particularly had in mind man's perennial tendency to use the State to attempt to improve situations through well-meaning policies that, for all their good intentions, actually create new problems. As Bastiat observed:

> [T]he relationship between work and reward is distorted, the laws of production and trade are disturbed, the natural development of learning is upset, financial resources and labor are misdirected, ideas are perverted, senseless claims are kindled, and chimerical prospects are opened up.

For his own part, Bastiat preferred to "trust entirely the wisdom of the laws established by Providence and, for that very reason, I put my faith in *Liberty*."

Freedom and truth are, thus, inseparable in Bastiat's mind. This leads him to three conclusions about the social order. The first is that there are moral truths that transcend time, place, and culture. The second is the link that right reason provides between freedom and truth. To be free, Bastiat understood that people must be given scope to choose. But freedom, for Bastiat, is more than simply free choice. When people choose freely to live in light of what Revelation and right reason tells us is the truth, Bastiat believed, they attain the type of self-ascendancy and mastery of the passions that orthodox Christianity has always proclaimed to be at the heart of true freedom

The third theme emerging from Bastiat's attention to natural law is the strongly anti-positivist dimension of his thought. In this regard, Bastiat set himself against the then-popular positivist doctrine (ultimately atheistic in its roots) that still persists in much contemporary thought: that is, the idea that a law is valid simply by virtue of having been legislated or decreed by the state. Bastiat primarily had in mind the attempts by European governments of his time to impede free trade in order to protect particular business interests from the effects of competition. In more general terms, Bastiat ascribed fully to Christianity's constant teaching throughout the centuries that laws decreed by the State, which directly violate the natural and divine law, may be generally understood as having no validity.

A Man of God, A Man for Others

Once one grasps the depth of Bastiat's antipathy toward positivism, it is impossible to view him as one who understood the world in terms similar to that of the many French Enlightenment thinkers. Unlike the often-deistic *philosophes*, Bastiat did not view God as a type of master watchmaker who, having designed the world as a clock, simply allows it to function on its own. Nor did Bastiat indulge in the fashionable juxtaposition of faith and science so characteristic of his own time. Instead, careful reading of Bastiat's writings illustrates that Bastiat was a man who grew passionately in love with the God who had graced humanity by implanting the light of reason within people. At no point did Bastiat's erudition as a scholar misled him into viewing the Creator purely in Aristotelian terms as a logically necessary but impersonal First Cause. "The deist," Bastiat noted, "has only about God the haziest of ideas." Instead, Bastiat had absorbed into his soul the essence of the message of Jesus Christ: that God is a Creator who so loved the world that He gave us His Only Son. "To be really communicating with God," Bastiat commented only days before his death, "man needs to rely on a Revelation. I myself took the matter the right way: I do not discuss dogma; I accept it."

The depth of Bastiat's faith as a Christian shines through in his regular invocation of Scripture, his awe at the willingness of the early Christian martyrs in Rome to die for the faith, his sense of the reality of evil, his awareness of the finality of divine justice, as well as his distinctly Christian metaphysical understanding of the nature of reason and free will, and the relationship between the two. The latter alone puts Bastiat firmly in the camp of Aquinas and Grotius rather than that of Voltaire and Rousseau.

One may, however, contend that the Christian essence of Bastiat's thought and personality is most evident, not in his important discourses about the creative character of human intelligence but, rather, in a public letter that Bastiat addressed to his compatriots only one year before his death. In this text, Bastiat expressed his support of General Eugène Cavaignac's use of the military to crush the violent insurrection of Jacobin agitators, middle-class Socialist intellectuals, and the Parisian mob, against the Second Republic that replaced the ousted July Monarchy in 1848. But Bastiat also spoke of his resistance to "all measures that [he] found tinged with arbitrariness." He refused to yield to "impulses of wrath or hatred against unhappy and misled brothers, whose ignorance was often exploited by treacherous suggestions." The core of Bastiat's words of restraint that resound with respect for inalienable human dignity are to be found in the last line of the letter where he states:

> *Love is the whole of the law*—that maxim of the Apostle is as true for our times as ever, be it in politics or in morality.

For those who are convinced of the political, economic, and, above all, *moral* necessity of free trade, rule of law, and a limited State, these words are a gentle reminder of the reasons why it is important to argue for the maintenance and enhancement of these institutions. Neither the free market nor a constitutional order of law is an end in itself. The Christians who support such institutions should do so because of their conviction that the market and the rule of law provide people with the opportunity to use their creative intelligence, to take responsibility for themselves, and thereby to grow as persons.

The same words also contain a distinct message for those Christians who favor the free economy concerning *how* they should argue their case. Respect for the inherent dignity of every human person should discourage Christians from engaging in *ad hominum* arguments or from automatically attributing ill will to those who take a different view. Such an approach is simply not a matter of tactics or good manners. Rather, it is the mark of the Christian to be uncompromising about the truth and to speak the words of truth to others in a sprit of love. The life and thought of Frédéric Bastiat exemplify this way of proceeding.

—Leonard Liggio, Jacques Garello, and Samuel Gregg

Introduction

The Philosophical and Religious Framework of Frédéric Bastiat's Works (1801–1850)

The present anthology is intended to provide authentic quotations to classical liberals who want to dispel the misunderstanding and suspicion that separate them from too many Christians. This is an urgent task indeed, as the several forms of liberty—religious as well as economic, political, and intellectual—are closely linked. Properly, de Tocqueville wrote, "Despotism can govern without faith, but liberty cannot."

In the memory of his fellow citizens, for about the last hundred years, Frédéric Bastiat was little more than a polemicist—brilliant but strangely optimistic. (How could he maintain that "interests are harmonious"?) It was in the United States that he was rediscovered by Leonard E. Read and his Foundation for Economic Education. As a matter of fact, however, Bastiat holds an important place among the French classical economists of Christian creed, from Jean-Baptiste Say to Daniel Villey. His image in the minds of the cultured public has been updated by Florin Aftalion, who published Bastiat's *Oeuvres économiques* at the Presses Universitaires de France, and, prefacing a new edition of *La Loi*, wrote, "As a philosopher of Law and analyst of the State, Bastiat's contribution is of the utmost importance and a striking topicality."

In the following pages, Bastiat will appear as a reasonable philanthropist, a farsighted liberal, and a profound believer. His discussions are interesting and useful to us because he never remained in an ivory tower when studying man in society, the needs and reactions of whom have hardly changed despite our technical innovations. He always wrote in order to clarify some factual situation, to fight some deep-rooted error or delusion, and to open sound ways toward humane solutions.

As a notable of the provinces, he read widely, particularly the Physiocrats, in order to improve the agricultural methods of his tenants. He observed that the wine country where he lived—the Chalosse, south of Bordeaux—was becoming depopulated as a consequence of a tariff war between France and England. He learned that in Great Britain there was an active campaign against the Corn Laws and went to London to meet Richard Cobden and his friends of the Anti-Corn-Law League. His book and conferences on the subject earned him a wide audience so that, when the Revolution of 1848 occurred, he was elected to the Assemblée Nationale of the Second Republic. There he waged a lively polemic against Pierre-Joseph Proudhon, Louis Blanc, and other social reformers.

There is little doubt that the friendly cooperation of Frédéric Bastiat and Richard Cobden was a landmark in the history of Western political thought. The enlarging of Cobden's Anti-Corn-Law League into a broadly sketched philosophy of free trade won the attention and sympaty of the French intellectual elites. Bastiat's writings were even more widely read in Germany and Italy than in France, and were well-known across the Atlantic. When the French economist Michel Chevalier—a follower of the reformist Henry de Saint-Simon—went to the United States to study its railway system, he was converted to free trade by local admirers of Cobden and Bastiat. Later on, Chevalier became an influential advisor to the government and was promoted to draft the Treaty of Commerce, concluded in January 1860 between Queen Victoria and Napoleon III. The commercial peace between France and England set the trend for freer international trade that lasted to the end of the nineteenth century.

A valuable book on that period, titled *Richard Cobden, un révolutionnaire pacifique*, was published in 1939 by Charles Taquey. It was prefaced by another top advisor to French presidents, the philosopher of *l'Ordre Social*, Jacques Rueff. An ample quotation from that preface is in order here, as it stresses the enduring necessity of fighting privileges and monopolies camouflaged by "national protection."

> The problem existing in England when Cobden began his action did not differ much, in fundamental nature, from the problem now confronting the world at large. Agriculture was then perishing from a regime that intended to protect it while imposing heavy sacrifices on the citizenry. It harmed most severely the farmhands, tenants, and land owners— that is, the very people it ought to have safeguarded, who were its most ardent supporters as well as its most active defenders.
>
> In all the countries currently claiming to be democracies, the existing regime tends likewise to lower the well-being of the people while maintaining that its aim is to enhance it. Everywhere, these regimes have been established under the pressure of organized interests—individual interests or group interests, which their promoters succeeded in clothing with a veil of general interest....
>
> Of course, the evil is infinitely worse and more widespread in the world of 1939 than it was in the England of 1839. It has developed its political consequences: It has deeply hurt and debased man, who has lost, along with the meaning of freedom, the intellectual and moral qualities that alone enable him to deserve and keep his freedom....

> One can hardly be surprised that such a situation has prevailed. It is the result of industrial concentration and of the immense extension of association in every branch of economic activity. Powerful interests have thus been born and have succeeded in ensuring at the economic level a transposition of representative systems that have been devised and consciously set up at the political level....
>
> That evolution was supported by many forces that sincerely wished to improve the situation of the working classes, but a regime of representation of interests could not but help generate—through costlier production and Malthusian methods—the opposite result: a lowering of the standard of living of the people.

The student who has read Henri Bergson will be astonished to find in these selections a striking intuition of the "évolution créatrice," though Bastiat calls it "perfectibility," and explains it by the interplay of two "social laws" that no legislator ever made: natural responsibility and solidarity. Both phenomena are present in all human groups, in any place and at any time. With the help of human reflection, experience, and memory, the result is that men are always apprentices and that mankind is ever progressing.

Responsibility, as observed by Bastiat, is the plain fact that our actions will inescapably generate consequences for ourselves, consequences that may be favorable or unfavorable but that teach a lesson. Solidarity is the plain fact that we all benefit or suffer more or less directly from the actions of our fellow men and that we will react through approval or blame, reward or retaliation, when the consequences reach us. Bastiat notices that solidarity so understood is somehow a "reflected responsibility."

To Bastiat, such mechanisms are providential. The Creator intended to give man freedom, and thanks to these mechanisms, he made individuals monitors and rewarders of one another, thus setting up boundaries to their respective freedoms. And he provided for the perfectibility of persons as well as of society by endowing men with intelligence and memory. (The French poet Paul Valery would add: Language!)

Now, political institutions may either assist or hinder the operation of that providential system. Philosophical analysis implies as institutional corollaries, therefore, freedom of transactions and limitations on the State's duties and powers. Since mankind would have perished long before admitting, through sound reasoning, those wise principles, religion proclaimed commandments and prohibitions that ensured the needed safeguards (notably in the Judeo-Christian Decalogue).

The original feature of Bastiat's writings lies in his rationally argued picture of such a providential order (while leaving its proper role to Revelation). The "social laws" rule absolutely, and they generate structures of which one might say (with the help of Friedrich A. Hayek) that they "result entirely from human actions but not from human designs." Thus, providence has made progress possible without trespassing on human liberty.

Bastiat could not foresee that Pope John Paul II would advise men of goodwill to sublimate the phenomena of responsibility and solidarity into moral and civic virtues, but he did convincingly incorporate evil itself into (or better: annexed it to) the divine "economy." Evil is a dissuasive and limiting factor against our mistakes and our misdeeds.

Nonetheless, Bastiat was the opposite of a utopian. He was deeply aware of sufferings and injustices that could neither be healed easily nor without long indirect circuits, and he knew that their consequences would perforce harm innocents for generations, until (if ever) men stop giving in to the lures of cheating and plundering.

Only God can erase so many sins through redemption and judgment....

Frédéric Bastiat's premature death (he was only forty-nine years old) prevented him from achieving his life's dream: writing a *Harmony of Social Laws*, wherein he would have given a full-fledged picture of the philosophy that inspired and molded all his writings—whether about economics, or ethics, or politics. The seed of his convictions was planted during his years at the Benedictine College of Sorreze. Several professors of that renowned institution (a royal military college created by Louis XVI) were Freemasons of the Scottish Rite, which requires of its applicants a faith in God. Bastiat's father, and other members of his family, attended the meetings of a Lodge in Bayonne, to which they introduced him early in life. His name appears in the archives of the Lodge from 1821 to 1833, the year he began a political career as Justice of Peace.

Bastiat's meditative and very independent mind enabled him to articulate for himself a forceful synthesis of liberal economic science and Christian mentality. The kernel of his convictions might be found in his daring statement: "I believe that Evil ends up in Good, while Good cannot end up in Evil, so that, finally, Good must prevail."

In the following excerpts, the reader will meet many a formulation that has grown familiar to the present supporters of the free market and limited government. For instance:

—about the purely psychological nature of *value*, Bastiat refined Say's law, stating that in every transaction, people trade services for services (see p. 12 from VI, 564).

—about what Bastiat calls the "solidarity" of the world's economy, Ludwig von Mises and Hayek termed *catallaxy* (see p. 27–28 from VI, 620).

—about the mainspring of human activities, which Bastiat links with the feeling of personality, within a context that Mises defined as the impulse to *discard dissatisfactions* (see pp. 28 from VI, 570).

—about the *hubris*, or *conceit* implicit in every form of socialism, which Hayek has called *constructivism* (see p. 24 from V, 447 and p. 25 from VI, 634).

—about the global result of human interplay, resulting in a steady growth in the resources and knowledge, which Hayek analyzed as *cultural evolution* (see p. 23 from IV, 452).

One will see that Bastiat sought a minimal State (though less curtailed than that desired by Murray Rothbard—see pp. 25–26 from VI, 18). He will also see that, anticipating James Buchanan about "public choice," Bastiat depicts the subterfuge of diluting the cost of privileges among the greatest possible number of payers (see p. 29 from VI, 622).

The main contribution of Bastiat to the mental tool-kit of our times in the political field is very similar to what Ludwig Erhard named *Soziale Markt-Wirtschaft*; that is, that the free market is the surest way to real social betterment and a higher standard of living, in the long run, for both the rich and underprivileged.

Like Florin Aftalion, Henri Lepage had the highest praise for Bastiat because of his philosophical contributions (this in an afterword to a beautiful book of excerpts published in Brazil by Gilbert Fournier). To conclude our present survey, we can do no better than to summarize Lepage's penetrating remarks.

Says Lepage: Thanks to Professor Hayek, we know that the market is not only an efficient tool for "allocating resources" but primarily a discovery process leading us to information, knowledge, and new ideas we could not acquire without trading goods and services. That cognitive theory is the great contribution of Hayek to contemporary economic science, but we find already in Bastiat the same basic intuition, notably in his article "Justice et Fraternité." There the parallelism between the two thinkers is clear, but they differ greatly on another point: the philosophy of property.

Hayek's approach is positivistic. His starting point is that of an anthropologist wondering, *Why property? How did men come to such an idea?* His answer is bound to the cognitive virtues of social mechanisms grounded in freedom. There is no efficacy without an implicit value; for Hayek, the value of the market is in the fact that it was able to let vast numbers of people survive who could not have survived without it.

To Bastiat, property is a natural right, a right deriving from the nature of man. Socialists think that property was a creation of legislators. Bastiat places in opposition to that idea the logical and biological anteriority of property: It is as much a providential creation as the human persons themselves. The justification of liberty and property lies not in their economic efficiency but in an *ethical and normative* reflection growing from Bastiat's deep faith in the existence of a transcendental order.

Says Lepage: "In spite of the 138 years elapsed since Bastiat's death, his thought is blossoming again in the extraordinary rebirth, in our times, of the theme of Natural Right." And he refers to the "famous book of Robert Nozik, *Anarchy, State, and Utopia.*"

The text for the excerpts is *Oevres Complétes de Frédéric Bastiat*, second edition, seven volumes (Paris: Guillamin, 1862). The reader will notice a vocabulary and style denoting a great writer versed in the classics. Bastiat practiced the oratory of our revolutionary period, and some slight abridgement has been deemed necessary!

Finally, it should be noted that throughout this monograph, the word *liberal* is used in its classical European sense: pro-free market and limited government.

Now let us turn to some of Bastiat's most typical manifestations of that spiritual and liberal stance, seen in various aspects of his worthy—and all-too-short—existence.

—Raoul Audouin
March 1991

1 A Life of Study and Dedication to Liberty

Letters of a Young Man

What interests me most seriously is philosophy and religion. My soul is full of uncertainty and I can no longer tolerate that state. My mind refuses to admit faith, while my heart longs for it. Indeed, how could my mind bring together the grand ideas of Divinity and the childishness of some dogmas? On the other hand, how could my heart refrain from finding in the sublime morality of Christianity the proper rules of conduct? Yes, if paganism is the mythology of imagination, Catholicism is the mythology of feelings. What could interest a kind heart more vividly than that life of Jesus, that evangelic morality, and that mediation of Mary! How moving they are....

—From a letter to Victor Calmètes
September 1820; Tome I, 4

I confess, my friend, that the matter of religion keeps me in a state of hesitation, of uncertainty that begins to weigh heavily on me. How could one avoid seeing a mythology in the dogmas of our Catholic faith? And nonetheless, such a mythology is so beautiful, so consoling, so sublime that one might find it preferable to the truth. I feel that if I had in my heart a spark of faith, it would soon become a fire. Do not be surprised by what I say. I believe in Divinity, in the immortality of the soul, in rewards for virtue and punishments for vice. Therefore, how immense is the difference between the religious man and the unbeliever! My predicament is hardly bearable. My heart is burning with love and gratitude for my God, and I do not know a way to pay him the tribute of praise, which I owe him. He just barely occupies my thoughts in a dim manner, while the religious man sees open for him a road to follow securely. All the ceremonies of cult keep him in the presence of his Creator. And then, how sublime is that drawing closer of God and man, that redemption! How comforting it must be to believe in it! If it is an invention, Calmètes, how wonderful!

Besides those advantages there is another one: The unbeliever must necessarily construct a morality for himself and, to comply with it, he will need a high degree of perfection in his understanding and a strong will to conform to it. But he will never be sure that some reason will not appear tomorrow for him to build another system. The religious man, however, has his path set for him; he is nurtured by a divine and permanent rule.

—To the same, October 1820; I, 4–5

I think that I shall settle irrevocably into religion. I am tired of research that has led me nowhere and can lead nowhere. There I am sure to find peace and shall not be tormented by fears, even if I should be mistaken. Anyhow, that religion is so beautiful that I can easily suppose that love for it could bring happiness in this life.

If I so decide, I shall return to my former tastes: Literature, English, Italian would keep me as busy as before. My mind has turned dull, pondering books of controversy, theology, and philosophy.

—To the same, April 1821; I, 5

How Bastiat Came to
Publish a Book About Cobden

I lived in a remote village of the Landes. There we had a club—and the members of the Jockey Club would be surprised if I should show them the budget of our modest association.[1] Even so, mirth and witty eloquence prevailed among us; besides having fun, we had subscribed to a couple of newspapers and we seriously discussed politics. No wonder, then, if we were patriots and very suspicious of English foreign policy. Being as familiar with English literature as is possible in a village, I myself suspected that our newspapers were somewhat exaggerating when depicting the hatred supposedly nourished by our neighbors against the French nation; I would now and then give vent to my doubts, but I was always defeated by quotations from our journalists.

One day, with an angry look, our most anglophobic colleague held out a newspaper and said, "Read this, and judge." There it was printed that the British Prime Minister had concluded a speech with these words: "We shall not adopt that measure; if we should adopt it, we would fall, like France, to the last rank of nations." I became as inflamed as he was.

But, thinking it over, I said to myself: *It seems quite extraordinary that a minister, a head of the government—a man who, in his position, must devote the utmost care and self-control in his utterances—would indulge in insulting us wantonly, without any motive, provocation, or justification. Mr. Peel cannot think that France has fallen to the last rank of nations, and if he did think so, he would not say so in front of the whole Parliament.*

I decided to investigate this. That same day, I wrote to Paris, asking to subscribe to an English newspaper, starting back one month earlier. A few days later, I received some

---

[1]   The meeting place of French aristocracy in Paris, on Boulevard des Italiens.

thirty issues of *The Globe*, and quickly searched for the untoward sentence of Mr. Peel, and found out that he said, "We could not adopt that measure without falling to the last rank of nations." The words, *like France*, were not present!

That set me on the track, and later on, I had many occasions to uncover similar "pious frauds" in the way our reporters would translate. But reading *The Globe* taught me a lot more. I could follow, during two years, the thrust and progress of the [Anti-Corn-Law] League. In those days I was already an enthusiast for the cause of commercial freedom, but I believed that it had been a lost cause for centuries, as it was never talked about in my country—probably not more than in eighteenth-century China. Great was my surprise and joy when I read news of that important matter being *agitated* for, throughout England and Scotland, of a ceaseless succession of immense meetings, and of the energy, wisdom, and perseverance of the leaders of that admirable association!

But I wondered even more why the League would grow, expand, shed the light of understanding on Great Britain, and absorb all the concerns of ministers and Parliament, without our daily papers ever mentioning the fact!...

Thinking naively that the silence, once broken, would not persist, I fearfully endeavored to become a writer; I sent some articles about the League to *La Sentinelle* of Bayonne. But the papers in Paris paid no attention. I began translating some speeches of Cobden, Bright, and Fox, and sent them directly to Paris newspapers—they did not publish them. *Is it possible*, I said to myself, *that on the day when commercial freedom will be proclaimed in England, we should be surprised in such an ignorance? I have but one resource*: writing a book ...

—VII, 325–26

A Political and Spiritual Program

No approval could be more precious to me than yours, since our country and mankind have lost your illustrious father whom I revere also as my intellectual father. Among the leaders of his school still alive, I am also proud to have the approval of M. Charles Dunoyer. His articles in the *Censeur Européen* on the balance of power among nations, as well as those of M. Charles Comte, have long ago decided the orientation of my studies and even my political behavior.

More recently, the economic school has been partly obliterated by numerous Socialist sects intent on achieving the universal good, not in line with the laws of human nature but through artificial organizations born from their imagination, a baneful mistake that M. Dunoyer has fought with a perseverance that one might call prophetic.

I am currently devoting as much time as I can to a labor of love that I think will be useful, though it consists only of translations. There exists in England a great trend of public opinion in favor of commercial freedom; that movement is carefully hidden by our newspapers, and if, time and again, they cannot but mention it briefly, they misrepresent its inspiration and its far-reaching import. I would like to bring the evidence to the eyes of the French public, to show them that across the Channel there is a large, honest, and judicious party, ready to become the national party and to determine the politics of England, and that we ought to join hands with those men. The public would thus be enabled to judge if it is reasonable to wrap everything that is English in that savage hatred so stubbornly fostered by our press.

I expect other benefits from that publication. People will see therein the *partisan spirit* attacked at its root, the *national hatreds* sapped underneath, the theory of markets for goods depicted not with pedantic methods but under popular and striking forms. Finally, they will see in action that energy, that *tactic of agitation* which, when a genuine abuse is denounced in England, results in the possibility of foretelling the moment in which that abuse will fall.

—From a letter to Horace Say, son of Jean-Baptiste Say,
November 24, 1844; VII, 378–79

There is in this book one ruling thought; it looms over every page; it vitalizes every line. That thought is written at the very beginning of the Christian creed: I BELIEVE IN GOD.

If its argument differs from those of some economists, it is because they seem to think: We do not believe very much in God, as we observe that natural laws lead to disaster. We keep saying *laissez faire*, however, because we do not believe in ourselves, either, and we understand that all human efforts to stop the thrust of those laws would only hasten the coming of catastrophes.

If it differs from the Socialist writings, it is because these say in substance: We assert that we believe in God, but, in fact, we trust only ourselves—and we reject *laissez faire*, all of us declaring that our respective schemes are infinitely superior to those of Providence....

Responsibility and solidarity: mysterious laws, the cause of which is impossible to conceive without the help of Revelation, although we can appreciate their effects and their infallible contribution to the betterment of society; laws that, by the very fact that man is social, are linked together, intertwine, and converge, however conflicting at times; laws that one would wish to observe in their whole interaction—but science, with feeble eyes and uncertain gait, is confined to method, the dismal crutches that are its strength but reveal its impotence.

—From posthumous chapters of
Harmonies Économiques; *VI, 588*

To the Last Drops

If my little treatise "Sophismes Economiques" succeeds, we might follow up with another called "Harmonies Sociales." It would be very useful, as it would meet somehow the leanings of our times, eager to find some organization or artificial harmonies; it would show people the beauty, the orderliness, and the progressive principle included in the natural and providential harmonies.

—From a letter to F. Coudroy, June 5, 1845; I, 57

Starting November next, I will give a course (at the Ecole de Droit) on social economy, taking the word in our usual meaning of *harmony of the social laws*. I guess that such a course, addressing young men who have logic in their minds and warmth in their souls, will be of some effect. I hope that I shall create conviction and, at least, alert them to the works of the best authors. Now, if our dear Lord would still grant me one more year of strength, my pilgrimage on this earth will not finally be useless. Is not editing a magazine and teaching young people better than being elected to Parliament?

—To the same, August 1847; I, 78

I am grateful for the concern you kindly show for my health. It keeps on faltering. For the moment, I am suffering a great inflammation, perhaps an ulceration of both the tubes that bring air to the lungs and those that bring food to the stomach. The question is whether that ailment will disappear or worsen. In the latter case, there would be no way of breathing or of eating—a very awkward situation indeed. I hope I will be spared such an ordeal, but I am preparing for it through patience and resignation. Is there not an inexhaustible source of solace and strength in these words: *Non sicut ego volo, sed sicut tu.*[2]

... I begin to believe that the main idea I tried to spread is not lost. Yesterday, a young man sent me for my information a work titled "Essai sur le Capital." There I found the following passage:

> Capital is the distinctive mark and measure of progress. For progress, capital is the necessary and sole vehicle. Its special function is to promote the transition from value to gratuity. Therefore, far from adding to the "natural price," as people say, its constant role is to lower it ceaselessly

Now, that sentence encapsulates the most beneficent phenomenon among those I have endeavored to explain. In it lies the key to an unfailing reconciliation between the classes of proprietors and proletarians. Since that way of looking at the social order was not missed but adopted by others—who will bring it to the attention of multitudes better than I could?—I did not altogether waste my labor, and I can sing with less regret my *Nunc dimittis.*[3]

—To Richard Cobden, September 9, 1850; I, 188

---

[2] "Not as I will, but as thou wilt." Jesus' prayer in the Garden of Gethsemene (Matt. 26:39).

[3] The Latin name of the Song of Simeon, which begins, "Lord, now lettest thou thy servant depart in peace" (Luke 2:29–32).

II A Link Between Adam Smith and Friedrich A. Hayek

Economics for the Layman

What is capital? Some say that it is land, the source of all riches, which was grabbed by the few. Others say that it is money, that vile metal object of the cupidity that has shed blood throughout history. Let us examine how capital is formed, as a way to forming a sound notion of what it really is.

When Robinson Crusoe was stranded by a tempest on a desert island, he doubtless wished to build a hut, enclose a garden, mend his clothes, and make weapons. However, he realized that to engage in such works, he needed materials, tools, and, most of all, food supplies. He could not start working unless he had in stock enough game or fish....

Thus, he would often say to himself, *I am the greatest landowner and the most miserable of men. Ground is not capital for me. If I had rescued from the sinking ship a bag of gold coins, it would be of no avail to me.*[1]

---

[1] Here Bastiat makes a long story short: Crusoe actually reports that he "discovered a locker with drawers in it, in one of which I found two or three razors, and one pair of large scissors, with some ten or a dozen of good knives and forks; in another I found about thirty-six pounds in money, some European coin, some Brazil, some pieces of eight, some gold, some silver. I

My only and necessary resource is hunting. One thing only could allow me to shift to other occupations: catching a little more game every day than I need for that day, and so possessing some provisions. While feeding on that stock, I might make weapons that would help hunting be more profitable and would give me more free time to engage in long-term works.

Thus, *materials, instruments,* and *provisions* make up the capital of an isolated man; it is also the definition of capital for man in society. The capital of a nation is the sum of the materials, instruments, and provisions of the population. By *materials*, I mean those that result from work and saving. Without work and saving, materials belong to nobody. With them, they belong, of course, to those who made them and abstained from consuming them....

To produce anything in the world, one must be provided with a measure of either one or two of those means, or all three together. Now, if someone is working with materials, tools, or provisions saved by another, he will have got them through a previous agreement with the owner. Unless the latter intends to be generous to his own detriment, he will ask for a remuneration. If, for instance, Crusoe lends Friday a game animal he had reserved in order that Friday might spend the next day busy on some tool, it will be because Crusoe thinks that a day's hunting plus the agreed remuneration will be more advantageous than some other contemplated work, while Friday reckons that working a day at

---

smiled to myself at the sight of this money; 'O drug!' I exclaimed aloud, 'What art thou good for? Thou art not worth to me, no, not the taking off the ground; one of those knives is worth all this heap: I have no manner of use for thee; e'en remain where thou art, and go to the bottom, as a creature whose life is not worth saving.' However, upon second thoughts, I took it away; and wrapping all this in a piece of canvas, I ... let myself down into the water, and swam across the channel which lay between the ship and the sands...."

Arthur D. Skouten kindly gave me that quotation, adding that this episode is frequently cited in economic treatises to show that a person may loudly profess a certain theory but not practice it.

another job will yield more than a day's hunt minus the required gift....

In complex societies, it seldom happens that a lender has the very thing that the borrower wants. This is why the lender will convert his capital (materials, instruments, or provisions) into money, by means of which the borrower can acquire the special resource that he wants. The payment for capital lent under that form is called "interest."

Because most loans require such a double conversion of capital into money and of that money into another capital, people have grown accustomed to confusing capital and coinage. This was one of the most harmful errors in political economics. Money is simply a means of letting things—realities—change hands....

Proletarians, you are told that capital is dragging to itself most of the profits. Yes, it does, when it is scarce. No, it does not, when it is abundant.

You are told that capital competes with labor. This is worse than a mistake; it is absurd and ridiculous. A plenitude of tools and materials cannot harm labor; a plenitude of foods cannot frustrate needs.

Workers compete with one another; labor competes with itself. Capitalists compete among themselves; capital competes with itself. Such is the truth. But saying that capital competes with labor is like saying that bread competes with hunger, that light is an obstacle to sight.

Proletarians, if it is true that the only way to your welfare is an indefinite increasing of available materials, instruments, and provisions—of capital—what should you ask from society? That it ensures the most favorable conditions for that accumulation. What are they?

The first condition is *security*. When people are not sure to enjoy the fruits of their work, they do not work and save. In a state of uncertainty and fear, existing capital will hide, dissipate, or flee. New capital is not formed. Available provisions diminish, as well as the share of all, but first your own.

The second condition is *liberty*. Without initiative, capital does not progress in proportion to the number of would-be workers; destitution spreads. Even charity for the masses becomes a false remedy, because, however great its merits, it cannot multiply resources—as it is only through work that we are able to multiply loaves of bread.

The third condition is *thrift*. When all the yearly savings of a nation are dissipated by the foolish undertakings of government or the luxury of private people, capital cannot grow. Therein lies the real cause of pauperism.

—VII, 249–55

We [economists] believe that services are exchanged for services; we believe that the great aspiration is for an equivalence of the exchanged services. We believe that the greatest chance for that equivalence to be attained lies in its being pursued under the influence of liberty where anyone may judge for himself.

We believe that whatever hinders liberty will disturb the equivalence of services and exaggerate inequality, the undeserved opulence of some, the undeserved destitution of others—with a general depletion of riches, the fostering of hatreds, divisions, fights, and revolutions.

—VI, 564

We know and say that it is not true that liberty reigns among men today; it is not true that the providential laws totally exert their action. Rather, they operate slowly, painstakingly, to repair the disturbing operation of ignorance and error. Therefore, do not make the mistake of blaming us when we say, *Laissez faire.* We do not mean by that: Let people alone, even when they commit an injustice. We want to say: Study the laws of Providence, admire them, and let them operate. Discard the obstacles set in their way by misuses of force and guile. Then you will see actualizing among men the twin manifestations of progress: equalization combined with improvement.

—VI, 567

Two Systems Confronted: Restriction and Free Trade

Two economic doctrines oppose each other:

The one, which is dominant in legislation and opinions, sees the way of progress in the surplus of sales over-purchases, of exports over imports—in a word, what is called *balance of trade*.

The other, which we try to propagate, is the exact opposite. It presents the exports of a nation as the obvious payment of their imports. We deem that the essential goal is that each payment should be as small as possible for the largest possible amount of imports. Hence, our motto is: Let everybody be free to go and purchase goods wherever they are cheapest and sell where they are dearest. Is not that the way to give least and get most?

This latter principle is, naturally and spontaneously applied by people when laws do not prevent them from doing so. The former principle resorts to restrictive laws. It commits military forces called "customs officers" to reject foreign wares. But the complement of that system—exporting much—is not so easy.

As each government intends to hinder imports, how is it possible for anyone to export much? At the bottom of that antagonism lies a well-known and sad maxim: The profit of the one is the loss of the other. Now, exporting being the condition of progress, there remains the need to *conquer customers*. It means, the rule of the strongest or the slyest. Each group of people will do as much as they can—if a nation obeys the tenets of the restrictive system, those people are logically invaders—if they stop conquering, their moderation is nothing more than impotence.

It is important to notice that, if the restrictive system were true, the spirit of hatred, envy, antagonism, and domination would be unquenchable, being rooted in truth itself. But if the opposite doctrine were to succeed in winning the assent of minds, if each nation were to follow the same reasoning as the individual and say, "My advantage is in the quantity of what I receive and not in what I give out. My advantage is to buy cheap and sell dear. My advantage is therefore to let merchants be, and liberate all exchanges"—then, things would change radically. The nations would refrain from menacing one another, not out of generosity but out of minding their own interest.

Let us remember, however, that such an immense revolution cannot be the fruit only of libre-echange but also and mainly of a spirit of free trade. The former might obtain from a momentary mood of opinion or from extraordinary circumstances, but when a monopoly is so suppressed, the spirit of monopoly may still survive. The proof of this has been provided by what occurred recently in England.

The Anti-Corn-Law League was endeavoring to spread in the three kingdoms the spirit of free trade, but their aim was still far from being reached when a mysterious disease in vegetables destroyed a great many foods. The aristocracy, yielding not to persuasion but to necessity, decided to open the ports. This prompted Cobden to utter this just and sad statement: "It is something humiliating, which should properly belittle man's pride, that a black stain on the humblest of edible roots has done more for the freedom of trade than our seven years of work, dedication, and sacrifice." Nevertheless, the spirit of monopoly that had given in on that matter has continued to direct England's policies in foreign affairs.

—VII, 188–93

Individualism and Fraternity

I shall begin by declaring this quite frankly: The feeling of personality, the indestructible desire that man bears in himself to widen the range of his actions, to increase his influence, to pursue his happiness—in a word, the individuality—seems to me, the starting point, the motor, the universal spring to which, Providence has entrusted the progress of mankind.

No other feeling will have an influence on man comparable to that constant and powerful feeling of personality. We may differ in our concepts of happiness. We may search for it in riches, in power, in glory, in the terror we inspire, in the sympathy of our fellow men, in the satisfaction of vanity, or in the crown of saints—but we always seek happiness and we *must* seek it.

We must conclude, then, that individualism—understood as the feeling of personality exceeding its proper limits—is as old as the feeling itself. It is a sad truth, that generally men will give full rein to their sense of personality and, therefore, abuse it so long as they can do so with impunity.

I said "generally," as I am far from implying that the inspirations of conscience, natural benevolence, and religious prescriptions do not frequently prevent personality from degenerating into egoism. But one can state that the general obstacle to exaggerated developments of personality is not to be found in ourselves, but outside. It lies in the personalities who surround us, who will react when we hurt them and keep us in check....

Throughout history we see nations afflicted by war, serfdom, superstition, and despotism, all evidence of the selfishness of men who were stronger or more gifted than their fellows. Their feeling of personality has never returned to its proper limits through self-containment or obedience to moral laws. To curb it so, it was necessary that sufficient power and understanding spread throughout the multitudes.

However sad, it is true that *life is a struggle*, and will be a struggle as long as man will bear in himself that impulse, always prone to go too far....

The matter now is to see if the well-understood and permanent interest of one man, class, or nation is radically opposed to that of another man, class, or nation. If so, fraternity is only a dream, as it is not to be expected that each one will sacrifice himself to all others (conduct which would be of no avail, as it would mean sacrificing mankind to mankind).

—VII, 335–39

The Ruinous Nonsense of War

Everywhere, at any time, we see man considering work as the onerous side of his condition, and satisfaction as the compensatory side. We see him shifting as much as he can the strain of work upon animals, wind, or water—but also, alas!, on the strength of his fellow creatures when he is able to dominate them. Such is the origin of war....

When a man or a group is working, and another man or group waits until the work is done and then engages in plundering, a great amount of human effort is lost. Armed plundering requires effort—at times, considerable effort. Thus, while the producer devotes his time to creating sources of satisfaction, the plunderer devotes his in preparation for the robbing of them. But when violence is effected or attempted, the sources of satisfaction are not augmented. Plundered wealth can answer the needs of other persons but not of *more* persons; so that the efforts of the despoiler to prepare the plundering and the efforts he has not spent on producing, are lost for mankind.

Moreover, in most cases a progressive loss occurs also on the side of the producer: He is not likely to wait for the menacing raid without taking adequate precautions. And all those precautions—weapons, battlements, munitions, and drilling—are so much work to do—so many efforts forever lost, if not for the defender, at least for the well-being of humankind. If the producer calculates that, even with fortifications, he will not be able to resist the plundering, the loss of production will be worse still, as nobody is eager to produce when he fears being robbed....

Now, man has done even worse than plundering riches as soon as they are created. Because human abilities are productive tools, he has enslaved men themselves as a shortcut to appropriating their products.

—VI, 583–85

On the other hand, by studying the effects of men's peaceful actions on one another, we can see that men have converging interests; that the progress, morality, and wealth of all are conditioning the progress, morality, and wealth of each one—and thus, we shall understand how the feeling of individuality can be reconciled with the feeling of fraternity.

There is a condition affixed, however: that such conciliation not consist of a superficial declaiming but that it be clearly, rigorously, and scientifically demonstrated. Then, in proportion to the penetration of that doctrine in the minds of more people, together with a spreading of enlightenment and moral science, the principle of fraternity will spread.

—VII, 337

Must we take the word [*fraternity*] literally? It is true that nobody could live long if all the sufferings in the world would affect him as one that falls on his own brother. We all have duties to fulfill toward ourselves, our parents, friends, colleagues, and dependents. We have professional and civic obligations. For most of us, those duties will absorb our entire activity, and it is impossible that we should ever think of the general interest of mankind and aim directly at it.

Man's organization and perfectibility allow us to expect that, by the force of things, the interest of each will come closer and closer to the interest of all; that gradually, observation and experience will lead us to mind the commonweal and contribute to it. It might then happen that the principle of fraternity will grow from the very feeling of personality instead of seeming to be opposed to it.

Apart from the relation of parenthood and the spontaneous deeds of benevolence and abnegation, I believe that we can say that the whole of economy in society rests on voluntary exchanges of services.

—VII, 340

III   A Loyal and Farsighted Parliamentarian

Declaration of Principles in 1849

Dear Compatriots,

You gave me a mandate that is drawing to its end. I fulfilled it in the same spirit that made you give it to me. Remember the polls of 1848: What did you want then? Some of you were greeting the Republic with rapture; some had neither agitated for it nor wished it; still others were afraid of it. But with a very sensible resolution, you all agreed on a twin purpose: to maintain and lawfully experiment with a republican system and to bring it back to the road of order and security. History will state that the Assemblée Nationale was true to that program....

We soon perceived that we should have to resist a widely held and seductive opinion. Under the pretense of satisfying the people, it was proposed to invest the revolutionary government with inordinate powers: that it should suspend withdrawals from savings banks and the repayment of public bonds; that it should seize railways, insurance companies, and transport. The ministers were inclined to follow that way, which, to my eyes, is nothing else than *looting regulated by law and implemented by taxation*. I daresay that I contributed in sparing our country such a calamity.

However, a frightening collision was impending. The genuine work of private workshops was replaced by the delusive activity of the "national workshops." The populace of Paris, organized and armed, was the plaything of ignorant utopians and troublemakers. The Assembly, bound to dispel one at a time by their votes those misleading imaginations, foresaw the clash but could oppose it only with the moral authority you had conferred on your representatives....

Convinced that it was not enough to vote, and that it was necessary to show the masses the realities, I founded another newspaper, which I called *Jacques Bonhomme*,[1] for I intended it to use the plain language of common sense. It would ceaselessly call for the disbanding of the insurrectional forces.

The storm broke out on June 24. Entering the Faubourg Saint Antoine among the first after the fall of the formidable barricades barring its access, I carried out two difficult tasks: I rescued some unfortunate people from being shot, on doubtful evidence, as insurrectionists, and I further penetrated the area to participate in the disarming.

After the victory I faithfully supported the policy of General Cavaignac,[2] whom I consider one of the noblest characters that the Revolution has brought to the fore. Nevertheless, I resisted all measures that I found tinged with arbitrariness, for I know that any overbearing in success will endanger it. Self-control, moderation in every direction, such has been my rule of conduct in my parliamentary activity.

---

[1] The nickname of the French peasant since the Middle Ages.

[2] General Eugène Cavaignac (1802–1857) was the Minister of War in the first months of the Second Republic. He suppressed the insurrection in a three-day battle across the barricades, resulting in the deaths of some one thousand soldiers and approximately four thousand rioters. Fifteen hundred others were shot, and eleven thousand were imprisoned or deported.

Toward the same period, I suffered a chest illness that, because of the immensity of the Hall of Parliament, prevented my appearance at the tribune. However, I did not remain idle. The real source of the wrongs and dangers in society was, I thought, in a number of erroneous ideas that possessed the minds of those classes who enjoy the strength of numbers. There was none I did not fight, though I knew that an action directed at causes is always slow to have an effect and is often insufficient to prevent perils from materializing.

When ownership was attacked in its very principle by some who tried to pass legislation against it, I wrote a booklet: *Propriete et Loi.*

When some assailed the particular form of ownership consisting in the appropriation of land by individuals, I published the brochure *Propriété et Spoliation*—which English and American economists have deemed helpful in the difficult matter of land rent.

When some wanted to build fraternity on legal constraint, I wrote *Justice et Fraternité.*

One aroused labor against capital; another deluded people with the wild dream of the gratuity of credit; I published *Capital et Rente.*

Communism was overflowing; I fought it in its most visible materialization with my brochure *Protectionisme et Communisme....*

When I became aware that nearly every economic error that contaminated the country had its origins in a false notion of the functions of currency, I wrote *Maudit Argent....*

Thus, either in the streets through action, or in the minds through controversy, I took every opportunity, as far as my health would allow, to combat error, whether it came from socialism or communism, from the revolutionary or the conservative movements. This is the reason why I sometimes voted with the Left wing of the Assembly, sometimes with the Right. Those who have read my writings, in whatever period they were printed, know that I always hated partaking in systematic majorities or oppositions....

Security is certainly the most urgent need in our times and the most precious good in all times, but I cannot believe that it is possible to build it on a firm basis through the excesses of triumph, irritation, violence, and outbursts of revenge. The candidate that you will honor with your votes will not be the representative of a class but of all classes. He must not forget that there is great suffering, destitution, and blatant injustice across the country. Repressing, always repressing, is neither just nor even prudent.

Searching for the roots of suffering, while bringing to them all the remedies that are compatible with justice, is a duty as sacred as that of maintaining order. Admittedly, one must not compromise on truth, encourage chimerical expectations, or yield to popular prejudice, especially in the midst of an insurrection. But nobody should have expected that I would yield to impulses of wrath or hatred against unhappy and misled brothers, whose ignorance was often exploited by treacherous suggestions.

The duty of a Chamber Representative, elected by universal suffrage, is to enlighten those who suffer, to talk them into reasonableness, to listen to their needs, to convince them of our sympathy.

Love is the whole of the law[3]—that maxim of the apostle is as true for our times as ever, be it in politics or in morality.

Yours faithfully,

—VII, 255–62

---

[3] Cf. Romans 13:8–10.

A Prophecy Against Legislators' Conceit

Whoever—ignoring the fact that the social body is a set of natural laws, as is the physical body of man—dreams of creating an artificial society and arbitrarily manipulating family, propriety, justice, and human nature, such a person is a Socialist. A Socialist is not busy with physiology but with sculpture; he does not observe, he invents; he does not serve men, he uses them. He does not study their nature, he changes it, following the advice of Rousseau.

—IV, 452

If man had been intended by nature to live and work alone, his only law would be responsibility, but it is not so, for man is destined to be social. Rousseau was wrong when he maintained that man is by nature a perfect and solitary whole, and that the will of a legislator had been necessary in order to transform him into a part of a greater whole. Family, city, and humankind are gatherings to which man is necessarily related.

The idea—intrinsically false—that a legislator had invented society was pernicious in that it induced us to think that solidarity is created by legislation; and we shall soon see our modern legislators draw from that doctrine their power to subject society to a fictitious solidarity, operating in the reverse direction of natural solidarity.

Socialists never waver when resorting to despotism, because they proclaim the sovereignty of their aims. They disparaged responsibility under the name of individualism; then they proceeded to annihilate it and absorb it in the sphere of operation of a so-called solidarity, extended beyond the limits of the natural one.

The consequences of that perversion of the two great motors of human perfectibility are baneful: There is no longer dignity or freedom for man. As soon as he who acts no longer has to personally bear the consequences, good or bad, of his act, the initiative of any activity must rest upon society. Now, society speaks through the laws—that is, through legislators. Behold: Here are a flock and a shepherd, and even less: an inert material and an engineer.

—VI, 613

The same people who, falling in distress, would be ashamed to beg from their neighbors, get rid of any qualm, provided that the State intervenes. As soon as the request is not addressed to an individual's generosity and, instead, the State comes forth as a middleman in the operation, it seems that the dignity of the supplicant is safe, that mendacity ceases to be shameful, that a forcible levy is no longer an injustice.... Everybody intends to live at the expense of the State, and one forgets that the State lives at the expense of everybody.

—V, 447

The first impulse of the State will be to seize all the mutual-benefit insurance associations under the pretense of centralizing them; to make that move palatable, the government will allow those funds to receive resources drawn from the taxpayers. Later on, the State will begin to fuse all of them into a single association, subject to some uniform regulation. Then the workers will cease to look at the common fund as their own savings to be administered by themselves.

After a while, they will no longer consider the allowances in case of illness or unemployment as withdrawals from a limited provision gathered by their foresight, but as a debt of society owed to them. They will not admit that the latter might be insolvent, and they will never be satisfied with the compensations.... The State will find itself ever again compelled to ask for more subsidies from the budget, ... mismanagement will spread, and reforms will be postponed from year to year as usual, until the day of an upheaval comes.

—From an unpublished speech quoted in the Basque magazine Ekaina, *November 21, 1987, 36–37)*

The Proper Domain of Politics

The doctrine that places the moving force of society in the legislators and government results in imposing crushing responsibilities on them in matters where they ought to have none. If there is suffering, the fault is the government's; if there is poverty, the fault is the government's— Is it not the general and sole motor of society? If the motor is not good, it must be discarded and replaced by another....

—VI, 634

To say that the aim of law is to let justice reign, is to use a phrase that is not strictly appropriate. One ought to say that *the aim of law is to prevent injustice from prevailing.* For indeed, that which has a definite existence is not justice, but injustice. The former results from the absence of the latter.

—IV, 360

The State will always act through the means of force, imposing its services, and determining the services people must pay in return under the form of taxes. The problem then boils down to this: What sort of things have men a right to impose on their fellow men by resorting to force? I have no right to compel anybody to be religious, charitable, learned, or industrious. But I have a right to compel him to be just; this is the case in a situation of self-defense.

Now, there can exist, in a collection of individuals, no right that did not pre-exist in the individuals themselves. Therefore, resorting to individual force is legitimate only as a means of self-defense. Precisely because governmental action always implies resorting to force, such actions must be essentially limited to maintaining order, security, and justice.

Every governmental action exceeding that limitation is an usurpation of conscience, intelligence, and work—in a word, of human liberty.

—VI, 18–19

IV A Wholesome Social Philosophy

The Natural Social Laws Set by Providence

Every human action will irresistibly generate a series of consequences, good or bad, that will fall partly on the author and partly on his neighbors, sometimes on mankind as a whole. Thus are set vibrating, so to speak, two strings, the sounds of which deliver oracles: responsibility and solidarity.

—VI, 600

The whole of human society is made up of intertwined solidarities. This conclusion flows from the communicating nature of intelligence. Even those efforts without visible connections have a common outcome in an ever-ascending medium standard of living, through a huge treasury of resources and acquired knowledge, everyone unwittingly drawing from it and contributing to it.

Solidarity is the ceaseless exchange of thoughts, goods, services, and works, and the interaction of virtues and vices that mold the human race into a great unit and fuse those millions of ephemeral existences into a common, universal, and continuous life.

The element of society is man, a free force. Being free, man is able to choose, and when choosing, he can be mistaken; being mistaken, he may suffer. I shall say more: Man is bound to err and suffer, for his starting point is ignorance; he is confronted with innumerable and unknown paths, all but one leading to error.

—*VI, 620*

The perpetual longing of personal interest is to quiet the needs or, more generally, the desires, through satisfaction. Between both terms—which are essentially intimate and intransmissible—intervenes the transmissible means: effort.

Above this apparatus, there looms the faculty of comparing and judging: intelligence. But human intelligence is fallible. We can err in several ways. We may wrongly appreciate the comparative importance of our needs. In that case, if we act alone, we shall give our efforts a direction inappropriate to our well-understood interest. If we act in a social frame, under the law of exchanges, the effect will be the same: We shall let the demand and remuneration go to some kind of futile or harmful service, and we shall direct the flow of human work in that wrong direction.

We may also err by pursuing blindly some satisfaction that can only suppress a particular suffering at the price of incurring new and worse sufferings. There is hardly an effect that does not become a cause. We are granted the faculty of foresight so that we can grasp a series of consequences, but our foresight is often defective.

—*VI, 570*

Responsibility is the natural sequence that binds for the concerned, acting being, the act and its consequences. It is a complete system of punishments and rewards that nobody can escape and that nobody has ever set up. Its manifest reason for being is to decrease the number of grievous doings and to multiply the number of useful ones.

Our life is indeed a long apprenticeship. We learn how to walk after many falls; we learn through harsh and repeated experiences how to avoid heat, cold, hunger, thirst, excesses. Let us not complain because those experiences are rough; if they were not, we should learn nothing from them.

It is the same with moral behavior. The sad consequences of cruelty, injustice, violence, deceit, and laziness teach us to be gentle, just, moderate, faithful, and industrious. The experience is lengthy, but it is efficient.

Such being the nature of men, one cannot but acknowledge in responsibility the moving force specially in charge of social progress. It is the crucible in which experience is refined.

—VI, 601

Action flows from individuality, while the consequences overlap into communities. Now, it is evident that every man aims by his constitution to be happy and to avoid suffering. Therefore, the individual will tend to act in such a manner that brings the consequences to himself when they are favorable, and to others when they are not. As much as possible, he will try to divide the latter between a greater number of persons, in order that those wrongs be less visible and arouse lesser reactions.

When a man's habit harms his neighbors, a repulsion manifests itself against him. His behavior is criticized, blamed, despised. And since the need for consideration is one of the most powerful impulses, it appears that solidarity, through the responses it determines against wrong actions, will tend to restrict and suppress them.

—VI, 622

Thus, solidarity is, like responsibility, a progressive power, a system of reciprocal punishments and rewards, aimed at limiting evil and spreading good, and propelling mankind on the way that leads to its betterment. The operation of those laws, together with the gift granted to us of relating effects to their causes, will, by the very pain they inflict, lead one back to the path of good and truth.

Far from denying that evil exists, we acknowledge its mission in the social, as well as the material, realm. That mission will not be fulfilled, however, when an artificial solidarity is extended to the point of destroying responsibility.

—VI, 13

Natural solidarity manifests itself on a much greater scale, and through unsurveyable connections, when we consider relations among nations, or among generations of the same nation. War is an instance of it. We start fighting, destroying valuable resources; then we find a way to shift the cost of those destructions onto our descendants by issuing public loans....

—VI, 620

Restrictive commercial policies are another instance. Providence has set the means, both plain and unerring, to create among nations a dispersal of resources, a diffusion of knowledge, a solidarity resulting in a simultaneous progress. All those advantages are hampered by the restrictive system that tends to isolate peoples. The result is to intensify the difference of conditions among them, to prevent the leveling upwards of their standard of living, to stop the fusions, to block the counterweights, and to lock the nations into their respective superiority or inferiority.

—IV, 33

The Noxiousness of Ignorance and Presumption

Errors generated by the weakness of our judgment and the force of our passions are the first source of evil, as it pertains principally to the domain of morals. When error and passion are individual, the evil, too, is, in a measure, individual. Reflection, experience, and the impact of responsibility are the appropriate remedies. Errors of that kind, however, can take on a social aspect, and cause far-flung damage when systematized by the leaders of a country.

—VI, 571

When human institutions infringe on divine laws, not only error, but evil is the result; but this evil deviates and falls on people whom it should never have injured.

—VI, 4

Now, such is precisely the learning of many governmental institutions, particularly those created as cures for our social grievances. Under the guise of philanthropy, a solidarity is fictitiously developed among men, resulting in inertia and the weakening of responsibility.

Through an improper use of public compulsion, the relationship between work and reward is distorted, the laws of production and trade are disturbed, the natural development of learning is upset, financial resources and labor are misdirected, ideas are perverted, senseless claims are kindled, and chimerical prospects are opened. The results of such wild expectations are a huge waste of human resources and displacements of the population. Experience itself is deprived of any efficacy. To sum up, one ascribes to all interests a false foundation, arousing people against one another. Then one proclaims, "Behold! Interests are antagonistic; freedom is the root of all evils."

—VI, 83

The more centralized the decisions of the State, the more the natural responsibilities will be transformed into fictitious solidarity. The effects of wrong behavior are deprived of their efficacy as retributive and preventive sufferings because they will fall on innocents instead of on the wrongdoers.

—VI, 615

When the public is so misled (about responsibility and solidarity), the natural laws will miss the target. Suppose that a policy harms the mass, but the mass is convinced that they benefit from that policy. Instead of protesting, the public will applaud and ask for more. This occurs frequently. The reason is the following: A governmental decision generates not a single effect but a series of effects. It may often happen that the first consequence is indeed favorable and clearly visible—precisely the outcome aimed at. But the following repercussions will spread throughout the social body a disease that is difficult to identify and to relate to its origin.

—VI, 623

To Understand Reality and Spread the Truth

Leading public opinion, by a thorough discussion of causes and effects, back to the sensible direction that opposes disastrous measures, would be a valuable service to one's fellow citizens.... When a misguided public mentality admires what is despicable, penalizes virtue and rewards vice, supports what is harmful and discourages what is useful, such a nation is turning its back on progress and can be brought again to wisdom only by the dire teachings of catastrophes.

—VI, 624

Evil exists. It is inherent to human failing. It manifests itself in the moral as well as in the material domain, in masses as in individuals, in the whole as in parts. But, because the eye may suffer and turn blind, will the physiologist no longer see the harmonious device represented by that wonderful organ? Likewise, because the social order will never lead mankind to the fantastic harbor of an Absolute Good, will the economist refrain from acknowledging how marvelous is its organization, aimed at the growing diffusion of enlightenment, morality, and happiness?

—VI, 591

Granted that individual ailments cannot nullify physiological harmony, much less could collective wrongs nullify social harmony. But how could the existence of evil be reconciled with the infinite goodness of God? It is not up to me to explain something that I cannot understand. May I simply observe that such an answer should not be required from political economics or from physiology. Those sciences, being made up of statements of facts, will study man as he is, without auditing God for his unfathomable secrets.

Hence, I shall repeat that in my writings I am not concerned with perfection but with indefinite betterment.

—VI, 594

I trust entirely the wisdom of the laws established by Providence and, it is for that very reason, that I put my faith in liberty.

—VI, 12

V Christian Faith
Was the Keystone

A Religious Bedrock for Liberty

Harmony does not exclude evil, but it leaves to it only the ever-shrinking room opened to it by ignorance and the perversity of our weakened nature.

Young people, in our times, when a painful skepticism seems to be the result and punishment of the anarchy in ideas, I should feel happy if reading this book [*Harmonies Economique*] could bring to your lips—in that realm of ideas it deals with—those words that are not only a shelter but a force, since one could say they were able to move mountains, those opening words of the Apostles' Creed: I believe.

—I believe, not with a submissive and blind faith, for the matter does not pertain to the mysterious domain of revelation but with a scientifically reasoned faith as befits things left to man's investigation.

—I believe that he who arranged the material world was not to remain foreign to the arrangements of the social world.

—I believe that he was able to combine and give harmonious mobility to free agents, just as he could do with inert molecules.

—I believe that his providence is shining as clearly, if not more so, in the laws he ascribed to interests and volitions, as it is shining in the laws that he imposed on gravity and momentum.

—I believe that everything in society generates improvement and progress, even when society is at first wounded.

—I believe that evil ends up in good, while good cannot end up in evil, so that, finally, good must prevail.

—I believe that the insuperable social tendency leads men to a constant approximation of a common physical, intellectual, and moral level, together with a progressive and indefinite elevation of that level.

—I believe that it suffices for a peaceful development of mankind that social tendencies be undisturbed and left free to move ahead.

—I believe those things, not because I want them to happen or because it would satisfy my heart, but because my intelligence gives them a well-considered assent.

Young people, if ever you likewise say "I believe," you will eagerly want to spread your convictions, and social problems will soon be solved because, in spite of a common opinion, their solution is easy: Interests are harmonious. Hence, the solution lies entirely in this word: liberty.

—VI, 20–21

The Supreme Pontiff and the French Clergy

I have always thought that the religious question would again agitate the world. The positive religions of our times retain too much of the exploitation mentality and means to allow the unavoidable spreading of enlightenment. Besides, religious overbearing will experience an enduring and stubborn resistance because it is intertwined and mistakenly confused with religious morals, which are supremely needed by humankind.

Therefore, it seems that mankind will not easily be rid of this sad vacillation in history. On the one hand, people will denounce religious abuse and, in the heat of struggle, they will shake and weaken religion; and on the other, they will exonerate the abuses with the zeal of defenders.

Daily news shows that we are far from either an agreement or a separation of the spiritual and the temporal. Some say that a complete separation will solve all difficulties, but those who make such an assertion should first demonstrate that the spiritual and the temporal can really follow independent destinies and that the spiritual is not the master of all.

I want to emphasize here that we have in France fifty thousand persons who are very influential on account of their standing and have sworn an entire and gentle obedience to their spiritual leader who, at the same time, is a foreign prince; and that the temporal and spiritual are so intertwined in reality, that those persons can do nothing, even as citizens, without consulting that foreign sovereign, whose decisions are above discussion....

Is there a solution to the affairs of Rome? Yes, that a pope would appear who would say, "My kingdom is not of this world."[1]

—VII, 355

---

[1] Cf. John 18:36.

The world is full of decent people who would be
Catholics but would hardly dare to appear as such.…
When I meet a man who declaims in favor of Catholicism, I
ask him, "Do you go to confession?" And he bows his head.
In my opinion, the reason lies in the fusion of both powers
in the same leader. When the clergy have political power, it
is not the clergy who serve religion but religion that serves
the clergy.

—VII, 359

You wish to know my position [as candidate—Raoul
Audouin] concerning the salary paid to the clergy. It is
true that I wrote that every believer should freely contribute
his share to the sustenance of the creed that he professes.
My ideal is universal justice. The relationship between
Church and State does not seem to me grounded in justice.
On the one hand, Roman Catholics are compelled to finance
the Protestant and Judaic cults. On the other hand, the State
takes advantage of its providing for your budget to interfere
in clerical matters. It has its say on the nomination of bish-
ops, canons, and deans. And to be sure, the Republic might
adopt, in the future, a conduct such as would offend your
feelings.

Moreover, I have faith in a future blending of all Christian
denominations or, if you prefer, the absorption of the dissi-
dent sects into the Catholic creed, but to achieve that, it is
necessary that no Church be a political institution. You cannot deny that the roles currently conferred on Victoria in the
Anglican Church and on Nicholas in the Russian Orthodox
Church, create severe hindrances to the gathering of the
whole flock under the same shepherd.

If it were up to me, I should not violently bring about
a separation of Church and State, although such a separation
seems to me good in itself. But the fact is that public
opinion—which Pascal called "the queen of this world"—

currently rejects it. It is this opinion that one should first conquer.

The day will come, I think, when the very clergy will feel the need to recover their independence, through a new agreement with the State.

—From a letter to a churchman, 1848; VII, 351

In every matter, unity is the ultimate consummation, the aim toward which the minds of men will forever gravitate without reaching. If mankind succeeded in doing so, it would be the very end of all free evolution.

Not unity, but variance and diversity are at the beginning, the origin, the starting point, because opinions are perforce the more different when the treasury of proven truths is the smaller, that is, when science has created a general agreement on fewer points.

—VII, 361

On the Eve of the Last Stage

Sometimes I regret having drunk from the cup of Science or, at least, not to have simply studied the synthetical philosophy or, still better, the religious philosophy. One may then draw from it consolations for every circumstance in life, and we might still manage tolerably the time left to us to spend in this world. But a retired, solitary existence cannot fit with our doctrines (which, nonetheless, rule us with all the force of mathematical truth), for we know that truth has no power except through its diffusion—hence, the irresistible drive to communicate it, spread it, and proclaim it.

Although we are conscious of knowing the truth about the mechanism of society from a purely human point of view, we also know that truth evades our grip concerning the links between this life and that which comes after. And the worst of our situation is that, in those matters, we deem it impossible for us to know anything with certainty....

We have several priests of distinction here. Every other day, they deliver teachings of the highest order; I follow them regularly. Yesterday, the preacher said that in man there are two tendencies connected respectively with the Fall and with the Atonement. The second leads man to make himself in the image of God; the former leads him to make God after his own image. He thus explained idolatry and paganism and showed their frightening convenience to corrupted nature. Then he said that moral decay has rooted corruption into man's heart so deeply that he would forever keep leaning toward idolatry—even to the point of introducing it into the Catholic creed.

Apparently, he was alluding to a host of devotional practices that are an obstacle for intelligence to adhere to religion. However, if they so understand the facts, why do they not openly attack those idolatrous practices? Why do they not reform them instead of eagerly multiplying them? I regret that I have no acquaintance with that churchman, as I hear that he teaches theology at the Bordeaux Faculty, so that I could not discuss the matter with him....

After all, my friend, in the midst of the deep darkness that we are in, let us cling to this idea: that a First Cause, intelligent and merciful, imposed on us for reasons that we do not understand, the test of the hardships of life. Let it be our faith. Let us wait for the day that he will decide to set us free from the ordeal and introduce us into a better life. Let our hope be such. With those feelings in our hearts, we shall better endure our sufferings and afflictions.

—From a letter to F. Coudroy, at Les Eaux Bonnes
July 1844; I, 47–49

Ultima Verba

The Lord saw it good to bind suffering with our nature, and willed that, in our constitution, weakness be antecedent to strength, ignorance to science, effort to result, need to satisfaction, acquisition to possession, error to truth, experience to foresight.

I submit without protest to the Lord's decree, admitting moreover that I cannot imagine a better device. Seeing that he, through a system that appears at once simple and ingenious, provided the means for humans to come nearer and nearer to a common and higher level—that he so ensures, through the very action of what we call evil, the permanence and spreading of progress—I do not simply bow to that generous and powerful hand—I also bless, admire, and worship it.

—VI, 594

From the Notes of P. Paillottet on the Last Days of His Friend

Rome, December 20, 1850

He told me, "I intend to live and die in the religion of my forefathers. I have always cherished it, although I did not follow its external practices." (He used the words *to live* only to spare my feelings.) I reminded him that he had told me in 1848, speaking of Jesus Christ, "It is impossible to admit that a mortal could have possessed a knowledge of mankind and the laws governing it as profound as that present in the Gospel."

Toward the evening, he talked to me about Rome, under the religious point of view. "What impressed me most," he said, "is the solidity of the traditions of the martyrs. They are there, one sees them, touches them in the catacombs. It is impossible to deny them."

—I, xiv

December 22, 1850

This morning I saw him writing these lines in his prayer book: "On December 21, I confessed to M. l'Abbé Ducreux. On the 22nd again, and received the Holy Communion from the hands of my cousin Abbé Eugène de Monclar." Immediately after, he spoke of the sacrament that he had received, and in the same context he explained his religious ideas:

"The deist," he said, "has about God only the haziest ideas. He often forgets his God, or else he calls him a 'first cause' and feels no obligation to think of him anymore. To be really communicating with God, man needs to rely on a revelation. I myself took the matter the right way: I do not discuss dogma; I accept it. Looking around, I see that the most enlightened nations on this earth are in the Christian faith. I am quite at ease, feeling in communion with that part of mankind."

—I, xlvii

Bibliography

Primary Sources: Works by Bastiat
Dealing with Economics and Liberty

Bastiat, J. Frédéric. *Economic Harmonies*. Translated by W. Hayden Boyers. Edited by George B. de Huszar. Irvington-on-Hudson, New York: Foundation for Economic Education, 1968.

Written in the last year of his life, the essays in *Economic Harmonies* center on the compatibility of actors in the marketplace, much like Adam Smith's "Invisible Hand" concept. Bastiat contends that individuals' interests do not conflict with each other and that working toward the benefit of oneself does not impede upon others' pursuit of benefits. The relationship between capital, wages, and the benefit of society is a primary example used throughout the book.

______. *Economic Sophisms*. Translated and edited by Arthur Goddard. Irvington-on-Hudson, New York: Foundation for Economic Education, 1996.

Economic Sophisms keenly displays Bastiat's ability to argue logically while satirizing the arguments of his opponent. Bastiat explores the sophisms, or fallacies, in arguments favoring restricted trade, artificial prices, and limited competition. This work also includes the well-known essay "Petition of the Candlemakers," a parody in which candlemakers lobby the government to restrict "foreign" daylight competition from the sun.

————. *The Law*. Translated by Dean Russell. Irvington-on-Hudson, New York: Foundation for Economic Education, 1996.

Bastiat's last published work, *The Law* is a short book advocating liberty and limited government. Bastiat uses a moral argument to show how governments become corrupt and to demonstrate the cyclical effects of the reduction of liberties. Bastiat contends that as bureaucrats expand government, citizens are more likely to become dependent on the government for services and thus they will more readily yield their liberties. From this cycle, Bastiat developed the notion of "legal plunder," an absurd situation where the government taxes citizens to pay them back the money they were originally taxed.

————. *Selected Essays on Political Economy*. Translated by Seymour Cain. Edited by George B. de Huszar. Irvington-on-Hudson, New York: Foundation for Economic Education, 1968.

This is a collection of essays that studies the operations of the State in relation to the market, property, and the person. It includes well-known writings such as "Property and Law," "Justice and Fraternity," "The State," and "Plunder and Law," a treatise decrying taxes.

————. *Things Seen and Things Not Seen*. Translated by W. B. Hodgson. London: Cassel and Company, 1910.

In this piece, Bastiat explains how governmental bureaucrats plunder the unknowing citizenry through taxes, tariffs, and trade barriers (these are among some of the "things not seen"). This work is a strong foundation for both *The Law* and *Selected Essays on Political Economy* in that it offers insight into the duplicity of governmental actions. In many scenarios, the government acts with the best intentions for society, but the result usually includes the reduction of personal and economic liberties.

————. *What Is Free Trade?* Translated and edited by Alexander Del Mar. New York: G. P. Putnam and Son, 1867.

In this book, Bastiat contrasts the virtues of true free trade with the bureaucrats' belief that they can decide what is best for society. Del Mar's comments are helpful in applying Bastiat's anti-tariff arguments to early twentieth-century America.

Secondary Sources: Works Extracting or Critiquing Thought from Bastiat

Cairnes, John Elliot. *Essays in Political Economy: Theoretical and Applied.* London: Macmillan Press, 1873.

Cairnes focuses on the debate over the gold standard, extracting arguments from Bastiat, and particularly from *The Law*, with regard to the political economies of different forms of government.

Dixwell, George Basil. *Review of Bastiat's "Sophisms of Protection."* Cambridge, Massachusetts: J. Wilson and Son, 1883.

Dixwell's lukewarm review of *Economic Sophisms* notes both the strengths and weaknesses of Bastiat's stance on tariffs and protective taxes. Dixwell acknowledges the legitimacy of Bastiat's proposed policies but notes that the political realities of the world would make their implementation unlikely.

Dorn, James A. "Law and Liberty: A Comparison of Hayek and Bastiat." In *Critical Assessments of Contemporary Economists.* Vol. 3. New York: Routledge, 1991.

This piece outlines Bastiat's impact on Hayek and highlights the differences in each man's economic thought.

Garreau, Lorenzo. *Bastiat and the ABCs of Free Trade.* London: T. Fisher Unwin, 1926.

This work expands upon Bastiat's *Economic Sophisms* to advocate barrier-free trade.

Gibbons, Daniel. *The Sham of Protectionism.* Brooklyn: Daniel Gibbons, 1927.

Gibbons uses the reasoning of and cites examples from *Economic Sophisms* to argue against governmental protectionism. This work serves as a good complement to Henry Hazlitt's *Economics in One Lesson* as both books draw from Bastiat's logic to refute different economic fallacies.

Hazlitt, Henry. *The Conquest of Poverty*. Irvington-on-Hudson, New York: Foundation for Economic Education, 1996.

Using Bastiat's logic and examples from *Economic Sophisms*, Hazlitt investigates ways of reducing poverty with little governmental intervention.

———. *Economics in One Lesson*. San Francisco: Fox and Wilkes, 1996.

Hazlitt claims that this piece was inspired by *Things Seen and Things Not Seen* and calls his work a merely modernized version of Bastiat's book. He argues that because of their accuracy in predicting behavior and consequences, many of Bastiat's ideas make ideal models for economics. Hazlitt borrows Bastiat's analysis of fallacies such as the "Broken Window" and "Investing Versus Saving" to explain economic processes.

Hendrick, Robert M. *Frédéric Bastiat, Forgotten Liberal: Spokesman for an Ideology in Crisis*. New York: New York University Press, 1987.

This work reviews Bastiat's laissez-faire views during the rise of Socialist sentiment in France in 1848. Socialist programs were on the rise due to poverty, low crop production, and the bureaucrats' accumulation of power. Bastiat sought free-market solutions to such problems, and Hendrick applies these concepts to present economic conditions.

Marx, Karl. "Outlines of the Critique of Political Economy." In *Karl Marx, Frederick Engals: Collected Works*. Vol. 28. Translated by Ernst Wangermann. New York: International Press, 1986.

Marx responds to *Economic Harmonies* by disputing Bastiat's stand on wages and labor.

O'Donnell, M. G. "Economics As Ethics: Bastiat's Nineteenth-Century Interpretation." *Journal of Business Ethics* 12.1 (1993): 57–61.

This essay focuses on the moral aspect of economics and the ways in which Bastiat's ideas are steeped in ethics. It discusses the workings of markets and how Bastiat's concepts can naturally attain moral outcomes within the free-market system.

Rothbard, Murray N. "Classical Economics." *An Austrian Perspective on the History of Economic Thought.* Vol. 2. Aldershot, United Kingdom: Edward Elgar Publishing Company, 1995.

Rothbard's work attempts to emphasize the religious and philosophical influences on Bastiat's thought and the laissez-faire tradition as a whole.

Russell, Dean. *Government and Legal Plunder: Bastiat Brought Up-to-Date.* Irvington-on-Hudson, New York: Foundation for Economic Education, 1985.

Russell applies Bastiat's thought to modern American society. Issues of focus include taxation and regulation.

Tenney, Jack B. *Let's Try Freedom Again.* Hollywood: Standard Publications, 1954.

Tenney pulls themes from various works by Bastiat to analyze the ways in which liberty may be reincorporated into a regulated society.

Secondary Sources: Biographical Works on Bastiat's Life

Blaug, Mark. *Great Economists Before Keynes: An Introduction to the Lives and Works of One Hundred Great Economists of the Past.* United Kingdom: Cambridge University Press, 1989.

This work offers a valuable overview of Bastiat, offering biographical statistics as well as a historical account of Bastiat's ideas.

Cleveland, Paul A. "The Life and Work of Frédéric Bastiat: One Man's Call for Liberty." *Journal of Private Enterprise* 10.1 (1994): 35–52.

Cleveland's essay addresses the history of Bastiat's economic thought.

Currand, H. "Bastiat, Frédéric." *International Encyclopedia of the Social Sciences.* Vol. 2. Washington: Macmillan and Free Press, 1968.

This piece is a straightforward account of Bastiat's life and thought. The information presented is beneficial for a factual foundation that will be useful in understanding deeper readings.

Hayek, Friedrich A. "Frédéric Bastiat (1801–1850)." *The Collected Works of F. A. Hayek*. Vol. 3. Chicago: University of Chicago Press, 1991.

In this piece, Hayek delves into the life and thought of Bastiat, exploring the influence that he has had on today's economic studies.

Roche, George Charles III. *Frédéric Bastiat: A Man Alone*. New Rochelle, New York: Arlington House, 1971.

In this biography, Roche describes nineteenth-century France as the historical context for understanding Bastiat.

———. *Free Markets, Free Men: Frédéric Bastiat, 1801–1850*. Hillsdale, Michigan: Hillsdale College Press, 1993.

Roche's second biography on Bastiat focuses on how the French thinker developed his arguments in the context of a fashionable and revolutionary Paris. By detailing how Bastiat's satires of governmental laws, taxes, and officials earned him respect as a proponent of the free-market system, Roche portrays Bastiat as one of the earliest critics of socialism.

Russell, Dean. *Frédéric Bastiat: Ideas and Influence*. Irvington-on-Hudson, New York: Foundation for Economic Education, 1965.

A historical account of Bastiat and other free-market thinkers of nineteenth-century Europe, Russell's book explores the origins of Bastiat's ideas and those of his contemporaries and adversaries.